Daily Prayer Verses

February

Bill L. Sherley

Copyright © 2022 Bill L. Sherley

All rights reserved

No part of this book may be reproduced, or stored in a retrieval system, or transmitted in any form or by any means, electronic, mechanical, photocopying, recording, or otherwise, without express written permission of the publisher.

Cover image and artwork generated by Jasper Art

Table of Contents

Introduction 5

February 1 - Psalm 30:11-12 6

February 2 - Isaiah 55:12...............................8

February 3 - 1 Peter 4:13 10

February 4 - Proverbs 17:15......................12

February 5 - Psalm 98:9................................14

February 6 - Proverbs 14:21......................16

February 7 - Proverbs 15:1........................18

February 8 - James 1:5 20

February 9 - Philippians 1:18...................22

February 10 - Psalm 37:40..........................24

February 11 - 2 Corinthians 7:2..............26

February 12 - Luke 1:74...............................28

February 13 - Proverbs 16:7.....................30

February 14 - Psalm 112:8..........................32

February 15 - Proverbs 8:17.....................34

February 16 - Proverbs 8:21.....................36

February 17 - Matthew 5:5 38

February 18 - Jeremiah 29:13 40

February 19 - Matthew 26:28 42

February 20 - Matthew 18:4 44

February 21 - Proverbs 16:19..................46

February 22 - Psalm 37:23..........................48

February 23 - Proverbs 3:6	50
February 24 - 2 Peter 1:8	52
February 25 - Psalm 1:3	54
February 26 - Psalm 132:15	56
February 27 - Galatians 3:26	58
February 28(29) - Philippians 4:7	60
About the Author	62
Books in This Series	63
Books By This Author	65

Introduction

In a world where our days are filled with to-do lists, deadlines, and constant distractions, it's easy to forget the importance of spending time with God. Prayer and Bible reading are two simple yet powerful ways we can stay connected to Him. This book is designed to help you do just that – make prayer and Bible reading a part of your daily routine. Each day includes a different Scripture verse and prayer focus. We hope that as you spend time with God each day, you'll be encouraged and challenged in your faith journey. May He bless you richly as you seek to know Him more deeply.

February 1 - Psalm 30:11-12

Thou hast turned for me my mourning into dancing: thou hast put off my sackcloth and girded me with gladness; To the end that my glory may sing praise to thee, and not be silent. O Lord my God, I will give thanks unto thee forever.

Lord, I am so grateful that you have turned my mourning into dancing. I was so lost and felt like I had no hope, but you came and showed me the light. You put off my sackcloth and girded me with gladness, and for that, I will always be thankful. I will never be silent in my praise for all that you have done for me. In Jesus's name, we pray, Amen.

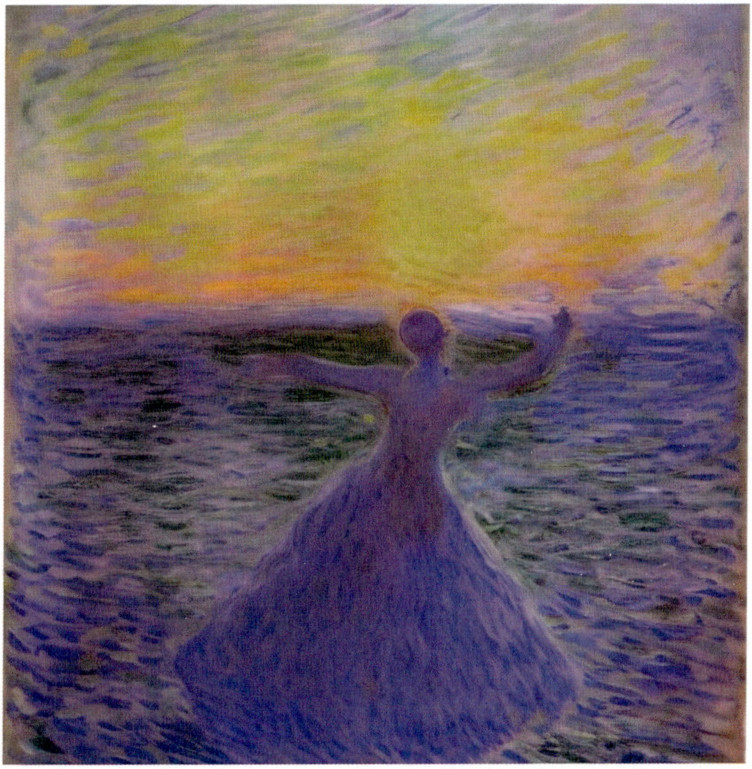

February 2 - Isaiah 55:12

For ye shall go out with joy and be led forth with peace: the mountains and the hills shall break forth before you into singing, and all the trees of the field shall clap their hands.

Lord, we praise you for the beauty of your creation. We thank you that we can enjoy the mountains and the hills that sing out your glory. We pray that as we go forth from this place, we would do so with joy and peace. That the trials of life would not overwhelm us, but that we would remember that You are always with us. In Jesus's name, we pray, Amen.

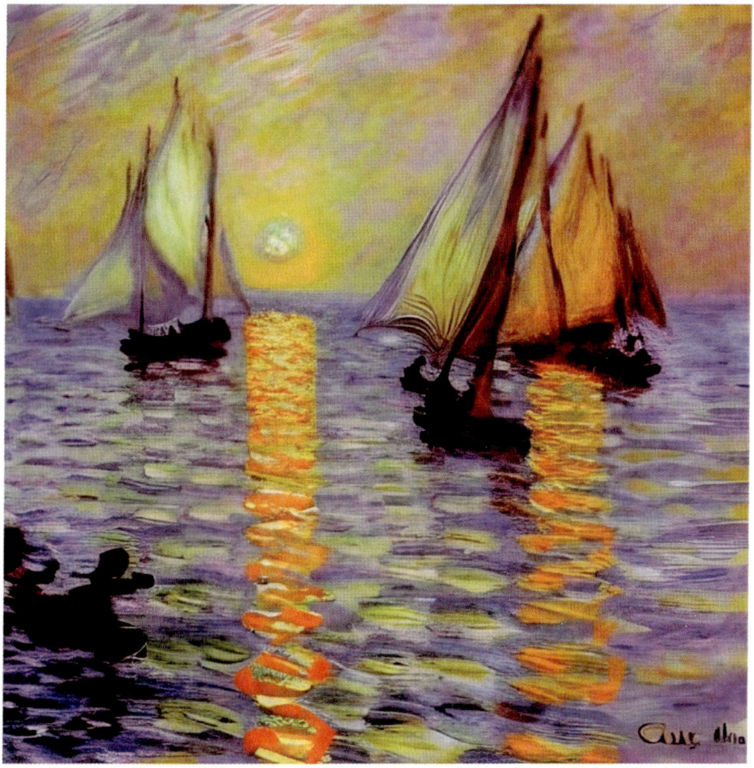

February 3 - 1 Peter 4:13

But rejoice, inasmuch as ye are partakers of Christ's sufferings; that, when his glory shall be revealed, ye may be glad also with exceeding joy.

Lord, we praise you for your glory and rejoice that we are partakers of Christ's sufferings. We pray that we may be able to withstand the suffering that is to come, and that we would be found faithful when he comes. We long for the day when we will be joyous beyond measure, knowing that all our sufferings are over. Thank You, Lord, for being our hope and our strength. In Jesus's name, we pray, Amen.

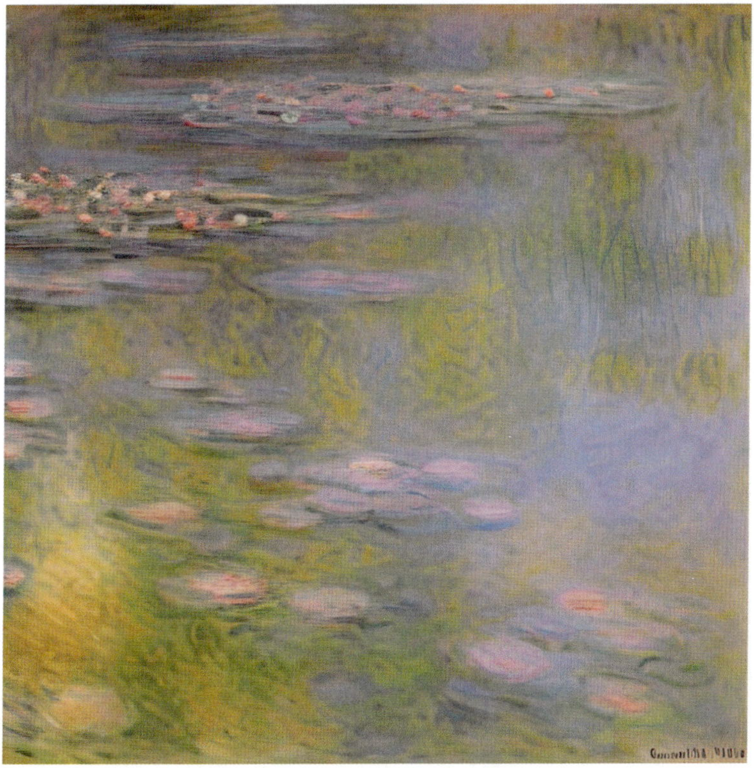

February 4 - Proverbs 17:15

He that justifieth the wicked, and he that condemneth the just, even they both are an abomination to the Lord.

Lord, we thank You for this Bible verse that reminds us to always be just in our dealings with others. We know that it is not always easy to do, but with your help, we can overcome any temptation to do wrong. We pray for strength and wisdom to always make the right decisions, and we ask that you guide our footsteps along the path of righteousness. In Jesus's name, we pray, Amen.

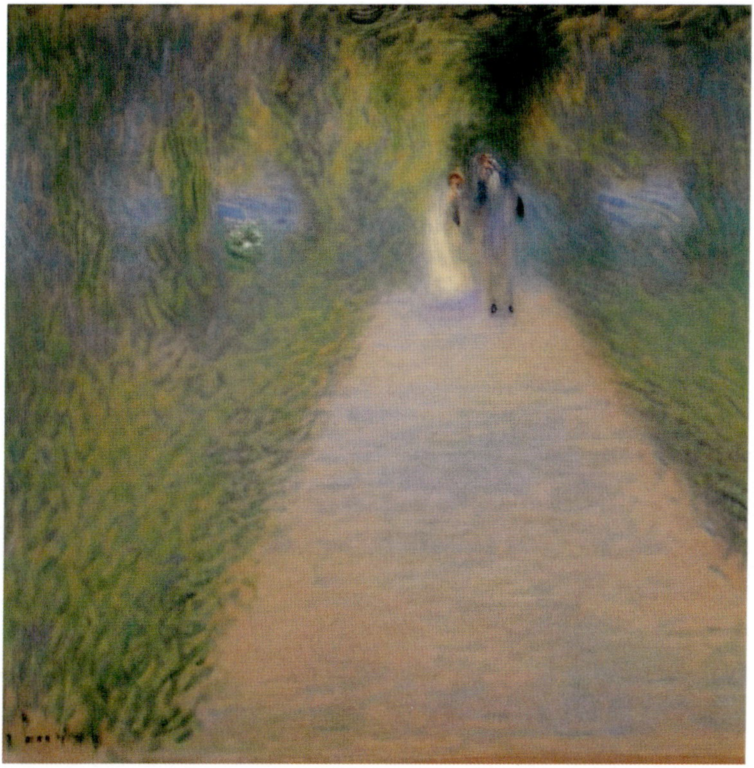

February 5 - Psalm 98:9

Before the Lord, for he cometh to judge the earth: with righteousness shall he judge the world, and the people with equity.

Lord, we praise you for your righteousness and justice. We pray that you would continue to judge the world with equity and fairness. We ask that You give wisdom to those who are in positions of authority, so that they may make righteous decisions. We also pray for humility among all people, so that we may be able to see your truth. In Jesus's name, we pray, Amen.

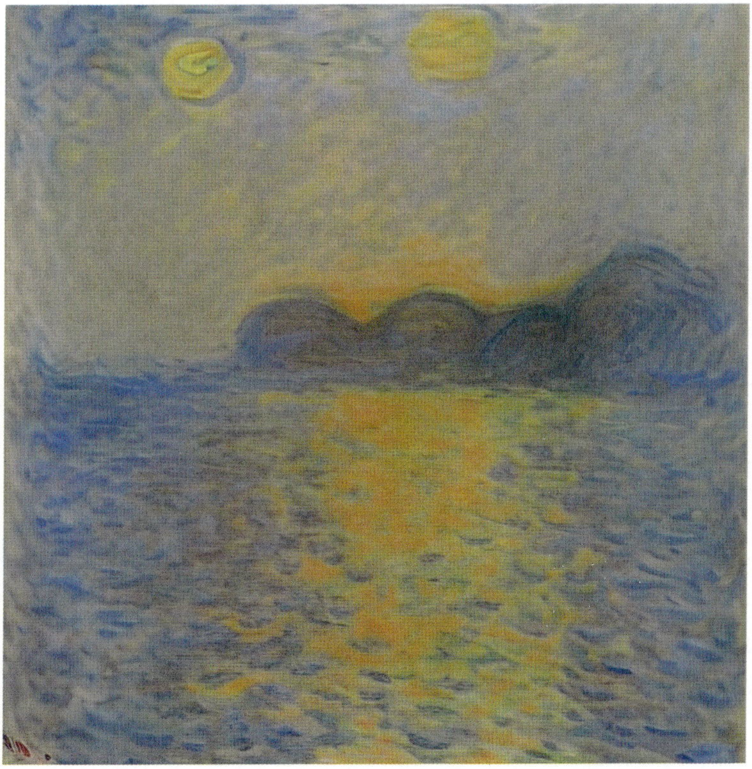

February 6 - Proverbs 14:21

He that despiseth his neighbor sinneth: but he that hath mercy on the poor, happy is he.

Lord, we thank you for your word. We thank you that you are a merciful God and that you love us unconditionally. We pray that we would have eyes to see the needs of those around us and a heart to meet those needs. We pray for your continued blessings on our lives, and that we would be a blessing to others. In Jesus's name, we pray, Amen.

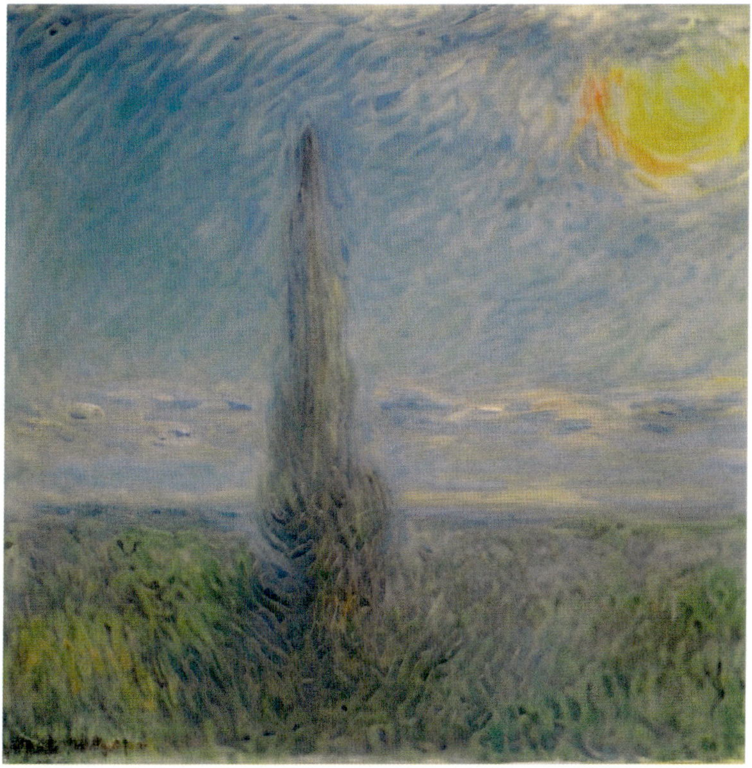

February 7 - Proverbs 15:1

A soft answer turneth away wrath: but grievous words stir up anger.

Lord, we pray that we would have soft answers that turn away wrath, and not grievous words that stir up anger. Help us to keep our tongues from evil and our lips from speaking deceitfully. We ask that you help us to watch our mouths and keep our hearts clean, so that we may be a testimony of your grace and mercy to those around us. In Jesus's name, we pray, Amen.

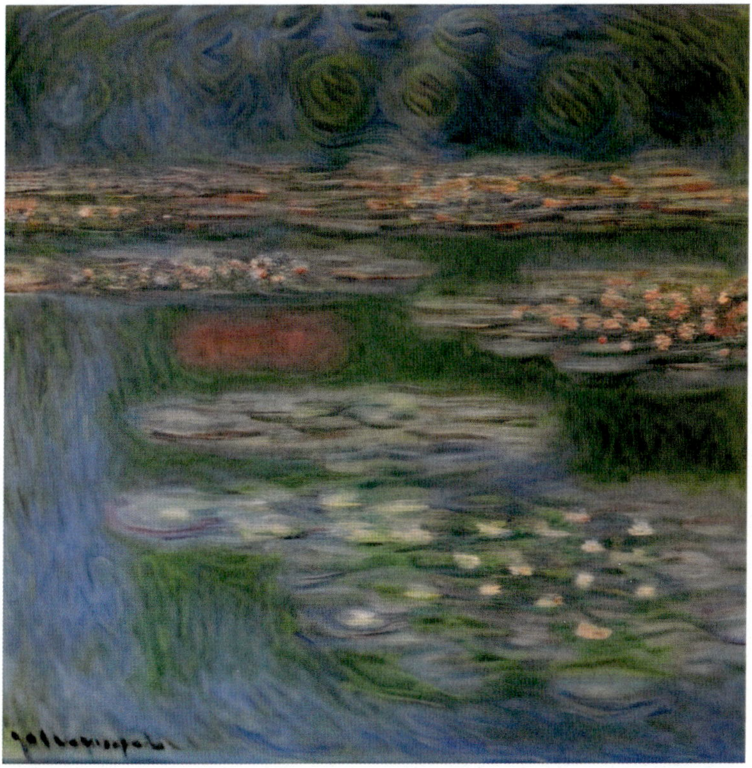

February 8 - James 1:5

If any of you lack wisdom, let him ask of God, that giveth to all men liberally, and upbraideth not; and it shall be given him.

Lord, we thank you for your Word. We praise you for your wisdom and knowledge. We pray that we would have the wisdom to understand it and apply it to our lives so that we may know how to live according to your will. We thank You that you are always ready to give wisdom generously, without criticism. We ask that You help us to grow in our relationship with you, so that we may better serve you and glorify your name. In Jesus's name, we pray, Amen.

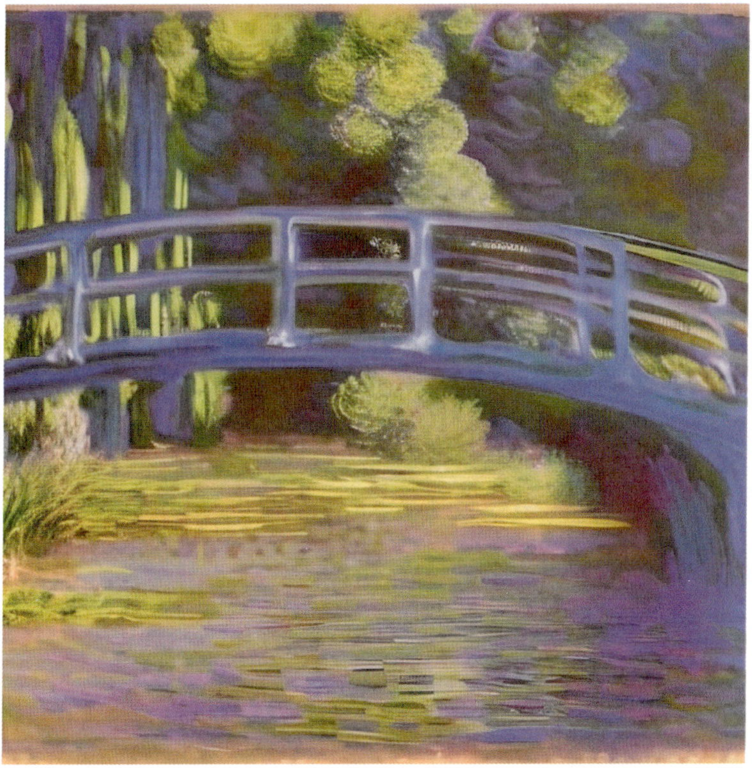

February 9 - Philippians 1:18

What then? notwithstanding,
every way, whether in pretence,
or in truth, Christ is preached;
and I therein do rejoice, yea,
and will rejoice.

Lord, we rejoice that Christ is preached in both truth and pretense. Help us to share your message with boldness and humility, speaking according to your will. May your Spirit guide our words, so that many may be drawn closer to You through Jesus Christ. In Jesus's name, we pray, Amen.

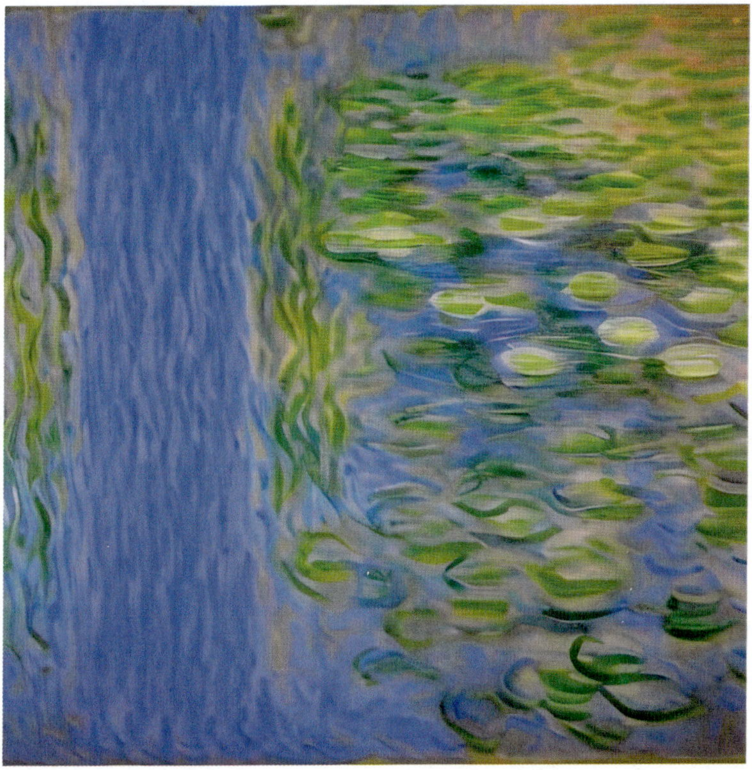

February 10 - Psalm 37:40

And the Lord shall help them and deliver them: he shall deliver them from the wicked, and save them, because they trust in him.

Lord, we thank you for your promise to help us and deliver us from evil. We ask that you continue to be our protector and shield us against wickedness. Help us to remember to trust in you when life gets difficult or when our faith is tested by the enemy. Grant us steadfast courage and strength as we seek after you with all our hearts. Give us the wisdom to know when and how to seek you and give us the faith to believe that you will never leave nor forsake us. Guide our paths so that we can remain blameless before you. In Jesus's name, we pray, Amen.

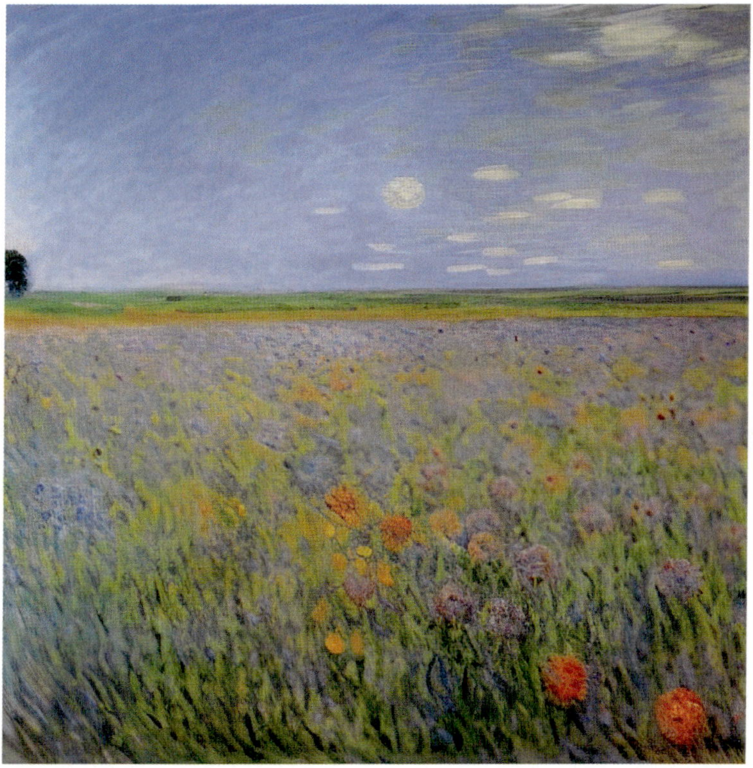

February 11 - 2 Corinthians 7:2

Receive us; we have wronged no man, we have corrupted no man, we have defrauded no man.

Lord, we thank you for your goodness in providing us with your Holy Word that guides us to seek and find salvation. We give glory to you for the teachings of 2 Corinthians 7:2, reminding us to lead a life of holiness and righteousness. Help us, Lord, to live our lives by these teachings, being mindful to not wrong, corrupt, or defraud anyone. Give us the strength and courage to always uphold our integrity without fail. We humbly ask for these blessings and more in Jesus's name, Amen.

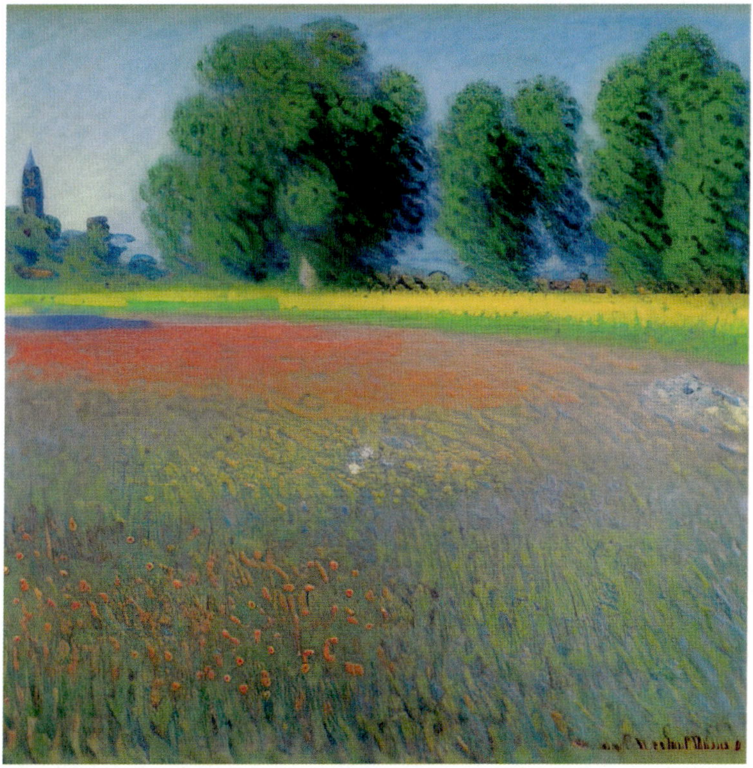

February 12 - Luke 1:74

That he would grant unto us,
that we being delivered out of
the hand of our enemies might
serve him without fear,

O Lord, we praise you for your mercy and grace. We thank you for the blessing of freedom that you have promised us in Luke 1:74. Guide us to serve you without fear, trusting always that you will protect us from our enemies. Help us to live a life obedient to your will and walking in your ways. Keep our faith strong and fill our hearts with courage, knowing you are always there to support us. May we have a heart of humility, filled with admiration and awe for your mightiness. In Jesus's name, we pray, Amen.

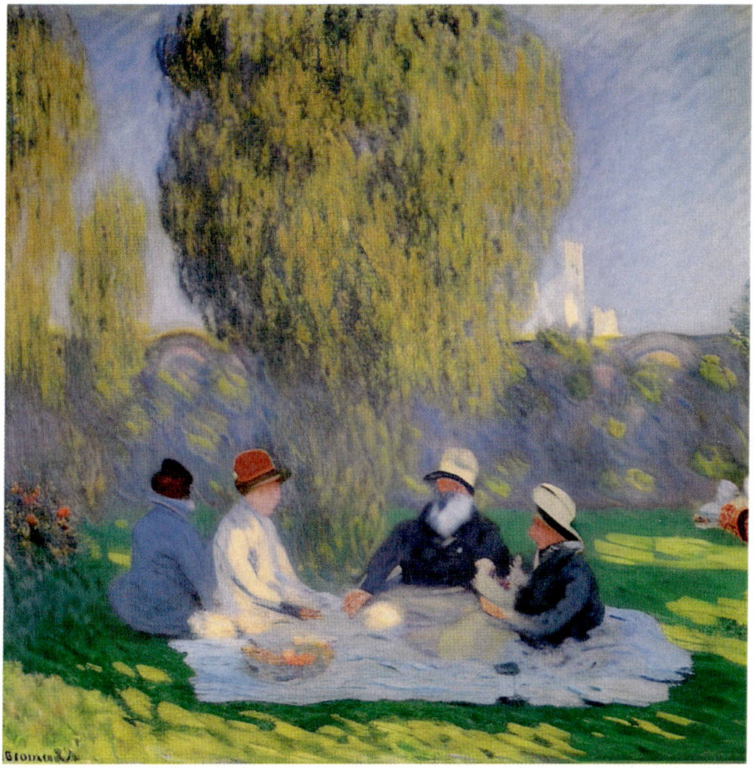

February 13 - Proverbs 16:7

When a man's ways please the Lord, he maketh even his enemies to be at peace with him.

Dear Lord, we thank you for reminding us that when our ways please you, even our enemies will be at peace with us. We praise you for your unfailing love and faithfulness, which can never fail. Help us to remain faithful and obedient to you, so that all those around us may experience the peace brought by your presence in our lives. Help us to always strive to seek your will and do what pleases you, regardless of our circumstances or the opinions of others. Give us wisdom and discernment to recognize when we are not pleasing you and for strength to make the necessary changes that honor you. In Jesus's name, we pray, Amen.

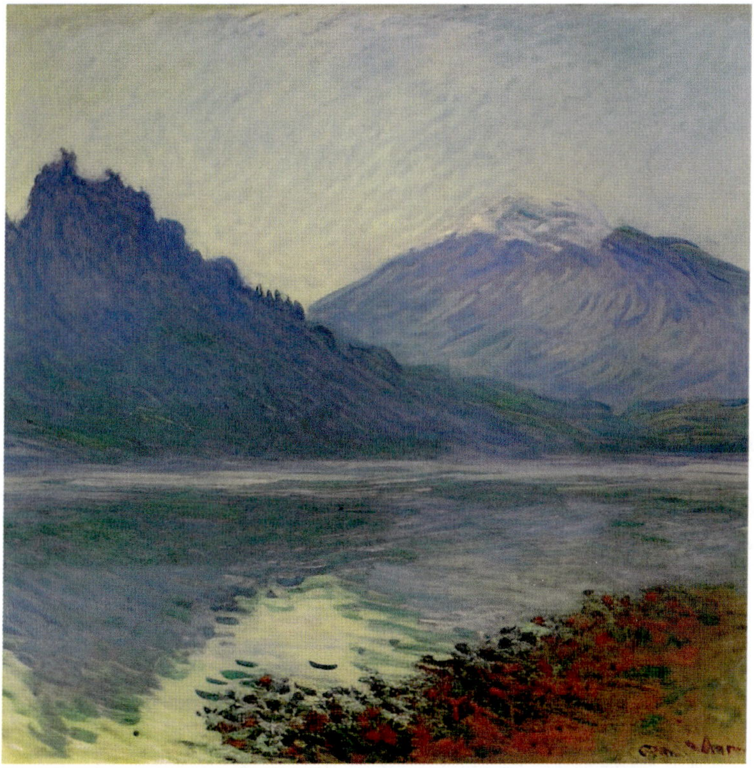

February 14 - Psalm 112:8

His heart is established, he shall not be afraid, until he see his desire upon his enemies.

Lord, we thank you for the peace that you bring us in times of distress. We feel secure knowing that your protection is a shield around us and that we have nothing to fear because our hearts are established in faith when they are fixed upon you. Help us to trust in your promises and not be afraid even when life's storms threaten. We know that your Word will prevail over our enemies, and we desire to see it come to pass. Strengthen us in faith, Lord, so that we can continue to strongly rely on you every day. In Jesus's name, we pray, Amen.

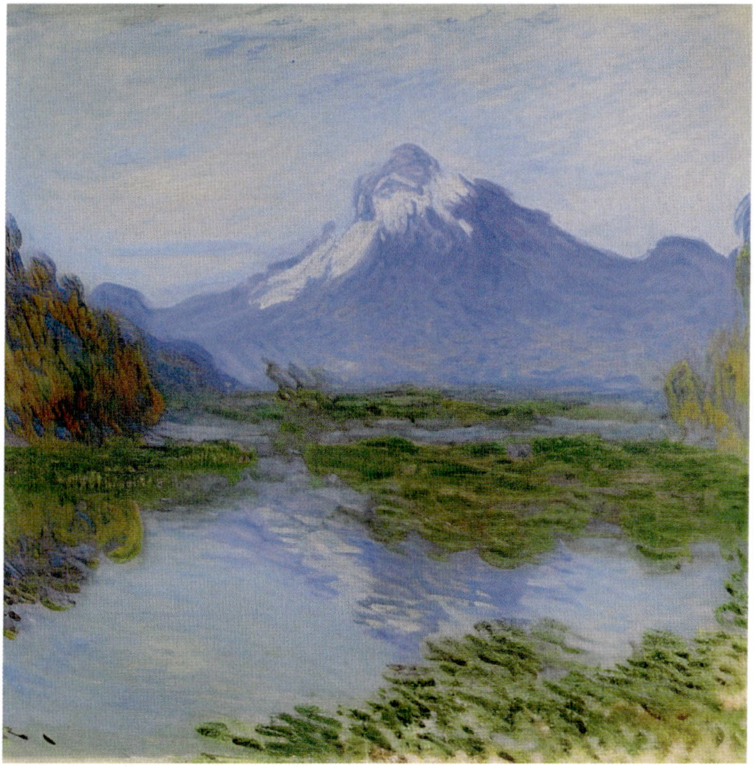

February 15 - Proverbs 8:17

I love them that love me, and those that seek me early shall find me.

Lord, we give thanks for the assurance found in Proverbs 8:17 that those who love you and seek you early shall find you. Give us the grace to love and seek after you with all our hearts so that we may find favor with you. Help us to trust in your promises and be obedient to your will. We ask that you open our eyes to recognize the opportunities You give us each day to proclaim your greatness and share in your grace. In Jesus's name, we pray, Amen.

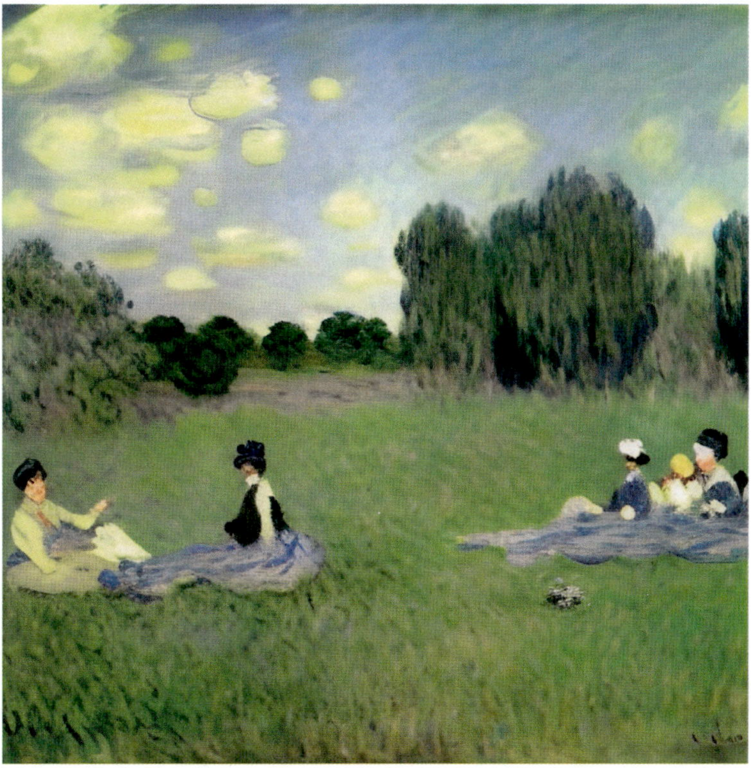

February 16 - Proverbs 8:21

*That I may cause those that
love me to inherit substance;
and I will fill their treasures.*

Lord, we thank you for your never-ending love. We thank you for your promises that those who love you will receive substance and be filled with treasures. Help us to remember the importance of loving you above all else so that our lives may be full of spiritual wealth beyond compare. Give us strength when times are tough so that we can cling to the hope of your promises. May we always be reminded that you are the source of all blessings and goodness in our lives. In Jesus's name, we pray, Amen.

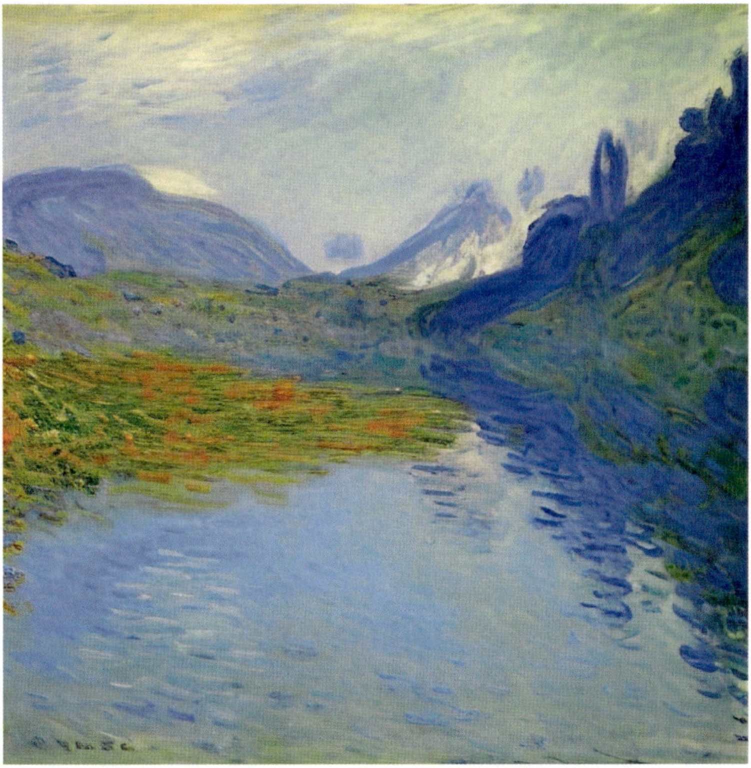

February 17 - Matthew 5:5

Blessed are the meek: for they shall inherit the earth.

Dear Heavenly Father, we thank you for showing us that meekness leads to inheriting the earth. We praise you for your mercy and grace. As we strive to be more like you, help us to become gentle and humble in spirit. Open our hearts and minds so that we may seek knowledge and understanding of what it means to inherit the earth. Guide us in our path, Lord, and help us to serve one another with meekness and love. In Jesus's name, we pray, Amen.

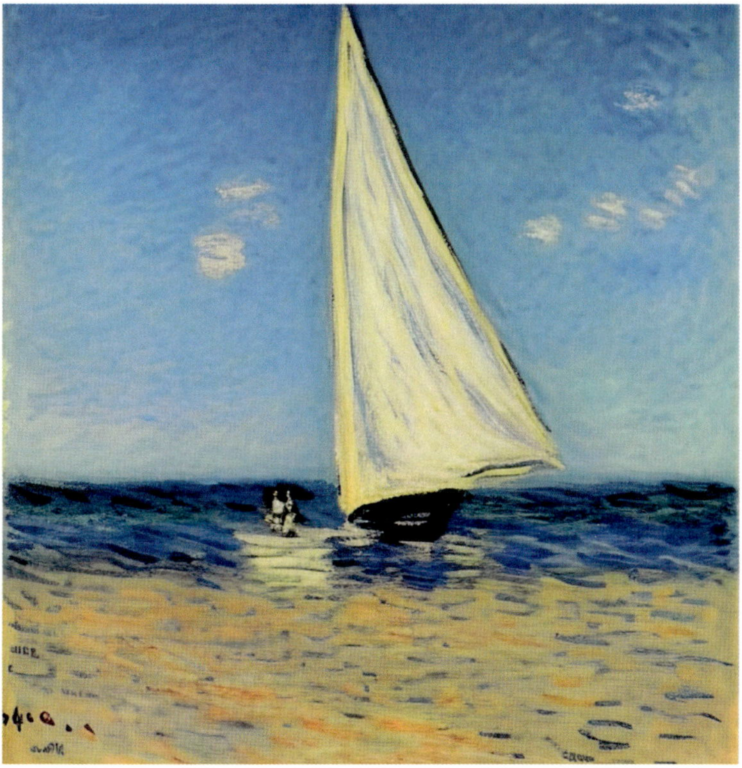

February 18 - Jeremiah 29:13

And ye shall seek me and find me when ye shall search for me with all your heart.

Father, we thank you for your Word that brings us strength and hope. We pray today for wisdom to seek you with all our hearts. Fill our lives with a deep longing for your presence, promises, and will. May we never forget that you are faithful and good in all things. Enable us to have firm faith in the assurance that you will be found when we seek you. Help us to always remember the joy of knowing your love and mercy. In Jesus's name, we pray, Amen.

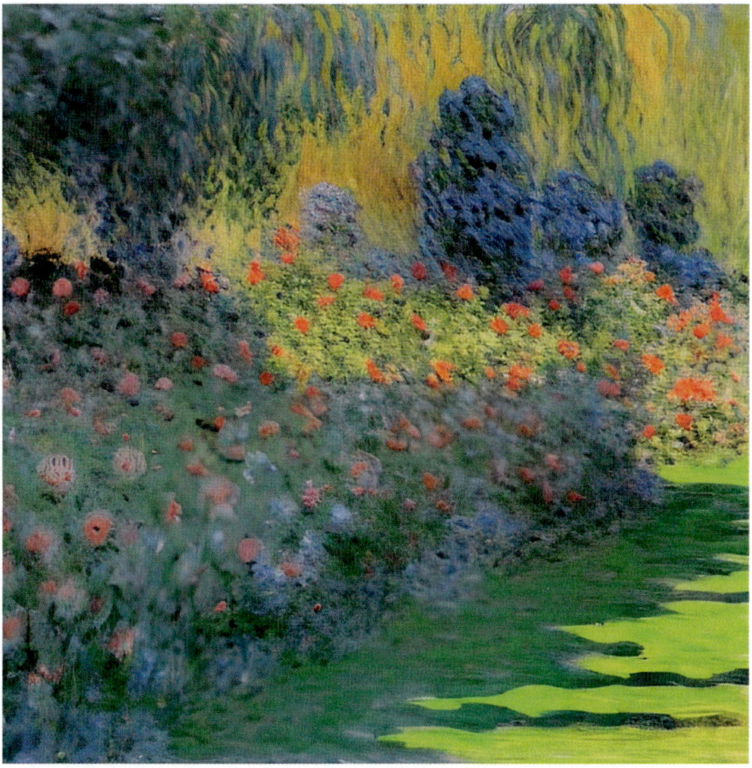

February 19 - Matthew 26:28

For this is my blood of the new testament, which is shed for many for the remission of sins.

O Lord, we thank you for your sacrifice. Help us never forget that through your blood, we are forgiven our sins. Give us a deeper understanding and appreciation of your grace, so that our hearts may be full of gratitude for what you have done for us. We humbly ask for guidance in living out a life that honors you. May our words and actions reflect your love for us. Help us to live a life worthy of the blood that was shed for us. In Jesus's name, we pray, Amen.

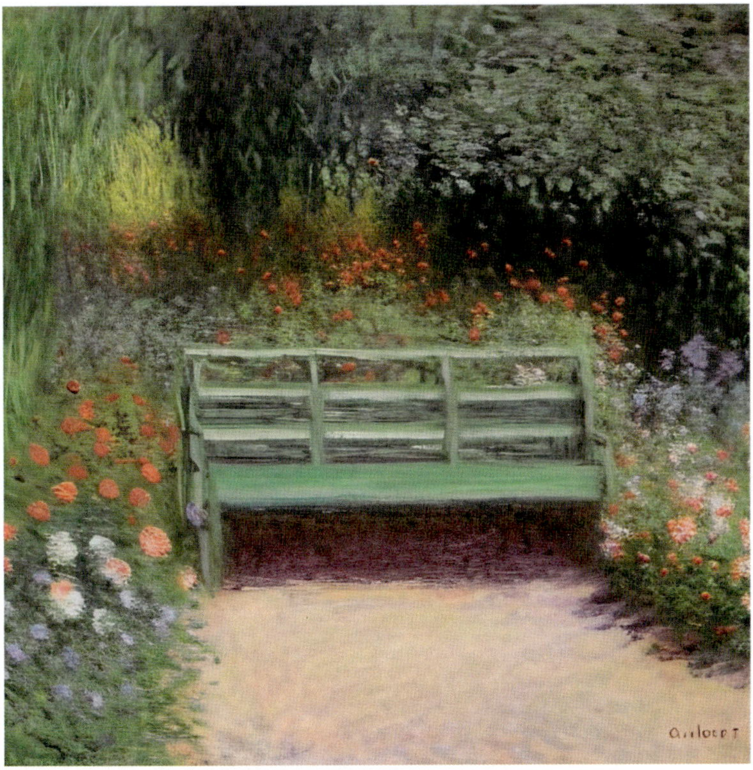

February 20 - Matthew 18:4

Whosoever, therefore, shall humble himself as this little child, the same is greatest in the kingdom of heaven.

Lord, we thank you for the reminder that humility is key to entering into the kingdom of Heaven. Help us to remember each day that only through humbleness and servitude can we become great in your sight. Open our hearts and minds to embrace this truth and act upon it. Guide us with your loving hand, so that we may always choose to be humble and serve you. Give us courage when facing obstacles, so that we may remain steadfast in our practice of humility. In Jesus's name, we pray, Amen.

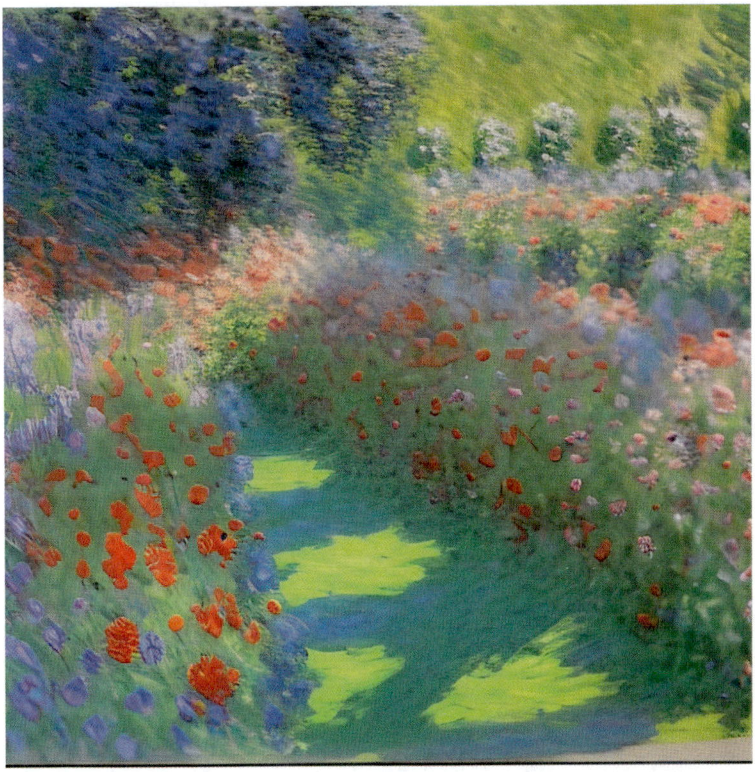

February 21 - Proverbs 16:19

Better it is to be of a humble spirit with the lowly than to divide the spoils with the proud.

Lord, we thank you for the reminder that it is better to be humble and of a lowly spirit than to be proud. Guide us in our decisions, Lord, and help us focus on being humble rather than self-serving. Open our hearts to recognize when pride is clouding our judgment and replace it with your wisdom. Give us strength and courage to live according to your will, even when our pride makes it difficult. Help us to recognize the beauty of being humble, knowing that you always have our backs no matter what. In Jesus's name, we pray, Amen.

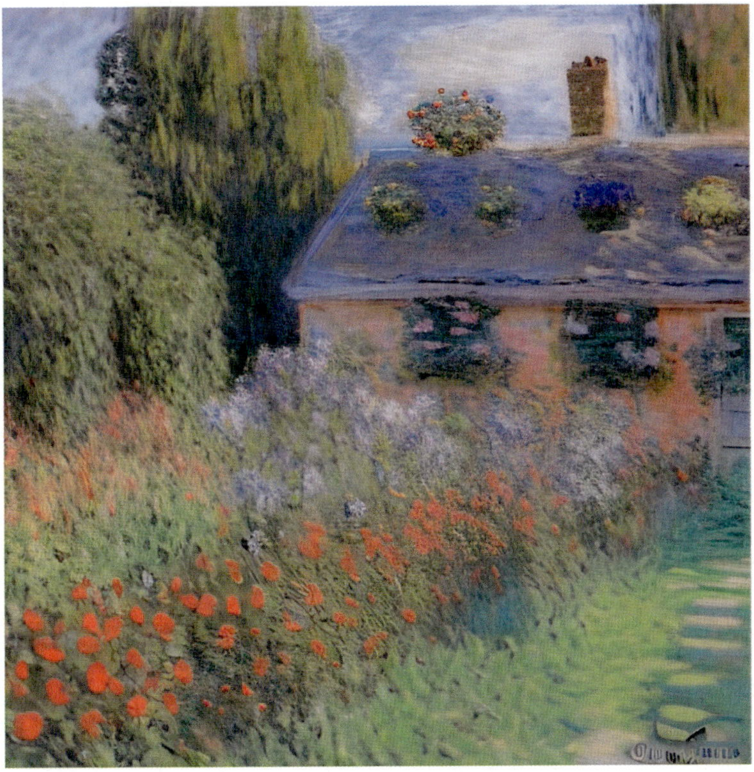

February 22 - Psalm 37:23

The steps of a good man are ordered by the Lord: and he delighteth in his way.

Lord, we thank you for your Word and the peace it brings. We are grateful that you order the steps of those who love you. Help us to follow in their paths, trusting in your will for our lives. Help us also to delight in our journey with you, even when times get hard. Remind us of your faithfulness, and that all we go through will work for good. Give us strength to continue in the paths You have chosen for us, and may we glorify your name with our lives. In Jesus's name, we pray, Amen.

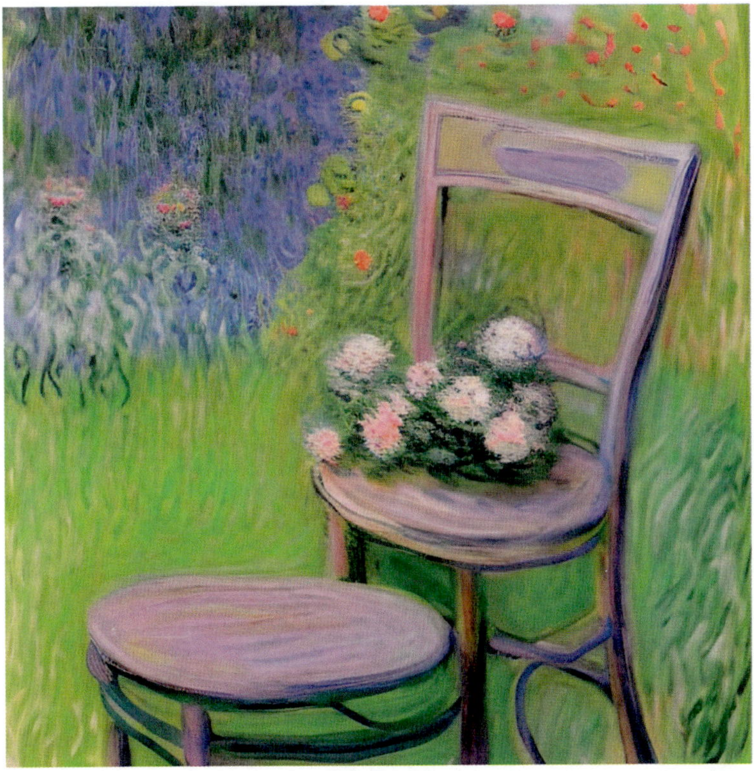

February 23 - Proverbs 3:6

In all thy ways acknowledge him, and he shall direct thy paths.

Lord, we thank you for your Word of wisdom and strength. We humbly ask you to direct our paths today as we acknowledge you in all that we do. Help us to live out this scripture and trust in the guidance you provide. We commit ourselves to seek after your will, leaning on your Word, and believing in Your promises. Let us practice in our lives the truth we find here that you are faithful and always look out for what is best. In Jesus's name, we pray, Amen.

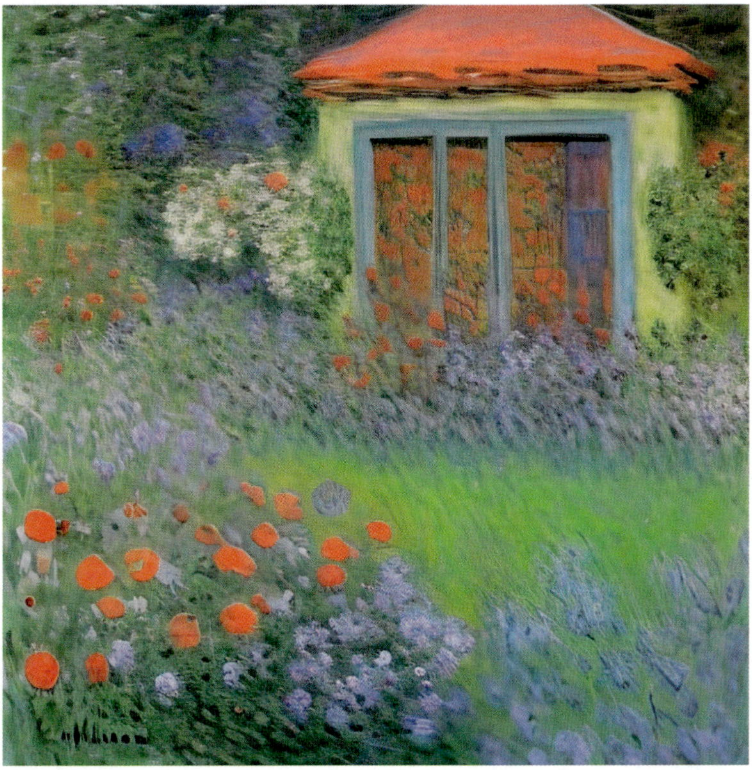

February 24 - 2 Peter 1:8

*For if these things be in you,
and abound, they make you
that ye shall neither be barren
nor unfruitful in the knowledge
of our Lord Jesus Christ.*

Lord, thank you for the knowledge of Jesus Christ and our ability to be fruitful in it. Help us to grow deeper in understanding as we seek your guidance and grace. Give us the strength to do what is required of us when called upon by you. Guide us on this path, that our feet will not stumble nor slip away from your will. Protect us from the deceptions of this world that try to lead us astray. Help us to stay focused on you and remember why we praise your name. In Jesus's name, we pray, Amen.

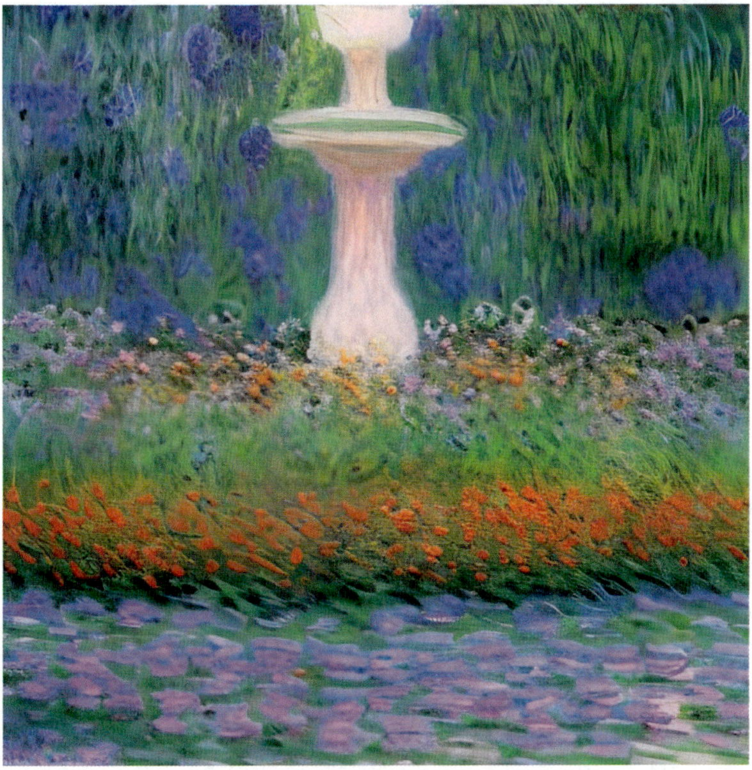

February 25 - Psalm 1:3

And he shall be like a tree planted by the rivers of water, that bringeth forth his fruit in his season; his leaf also shall not wither, and whatsoever he doeth shall prosper.

Lord, we thank you for the promise that those who follow you and your word will be blessed like a tree planted by rivers of water. We are humbled by your faithful love and mercy as we abide in you. Help us to trust in your perfect plan for our lives and allow us to bear fruit in season, even when times are difficult. Give us the courage to continue in your path and not be swayed by the world around us. Help us to remain hopeful and faithful, even when our leaf begins to wither. We ask that you make every endeavor of ours successful as we persevere with trust in you. In Jesus's name, we pray, Amen.

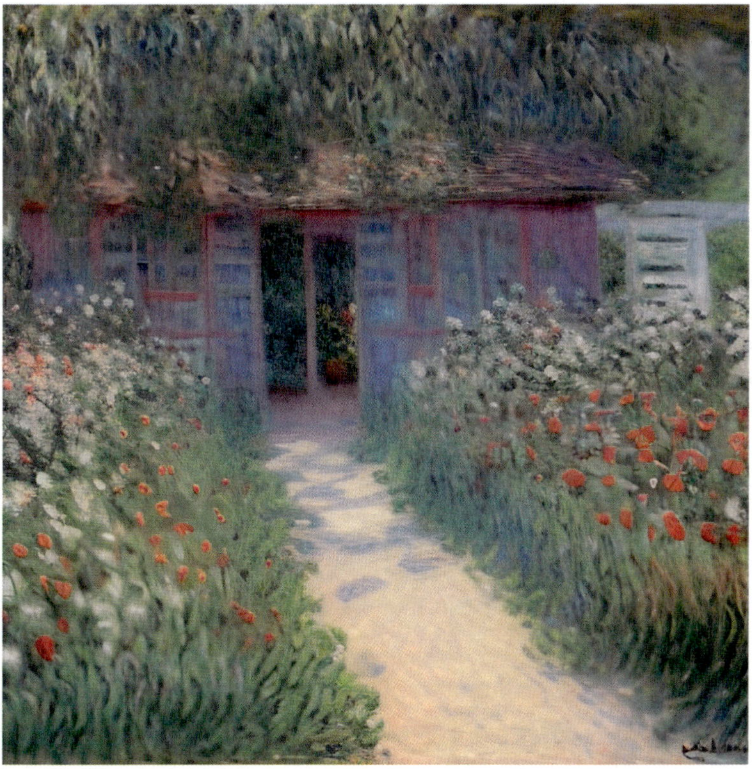

February 26 - Psalm 132:15

I will abundantly bless her provision: I will satisfy her poor with bread.

O gracious and loving Father, we thank you for your provision of the abundance that blesses us. We give you thanks for your mercy in satisfying the needs of those who are poor. We ask that you continue to provide sustenance and nourishment to those in need. Please bring peace, joy, and contentment into their lives as they rely on you. May we find hope and joy in your promises, knowing that you will never leave us nor forsake us. We are grateful to you for your steadfast love and grace. In Jesus's name, we pray, Amen.

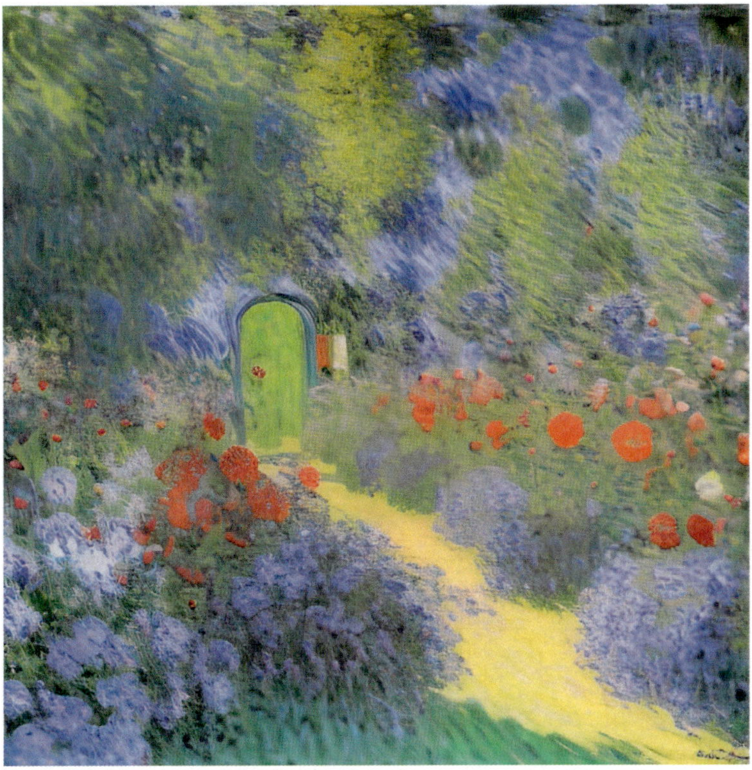

February 27 - Galatians 3:26

For ye are all the children of God by faith in Christ Jesus.

Lord, we praise you that through our faith in Christ Jesus, we are all children of God. Help us to recognize and claim our fatherly inheritance as sons and daughters of God and accept with gratitude the privileges it entails. May we always show gratitude to you and make choices that reflect our identity as your beloved children. Give us strength and courage to remain faithful to your word, no matter the trials or temptations we may face. Help us draw deeper into this wonderful fellowship with you so that we can be a blessing to others in turn. In Jesus's name, we pray, Amen.

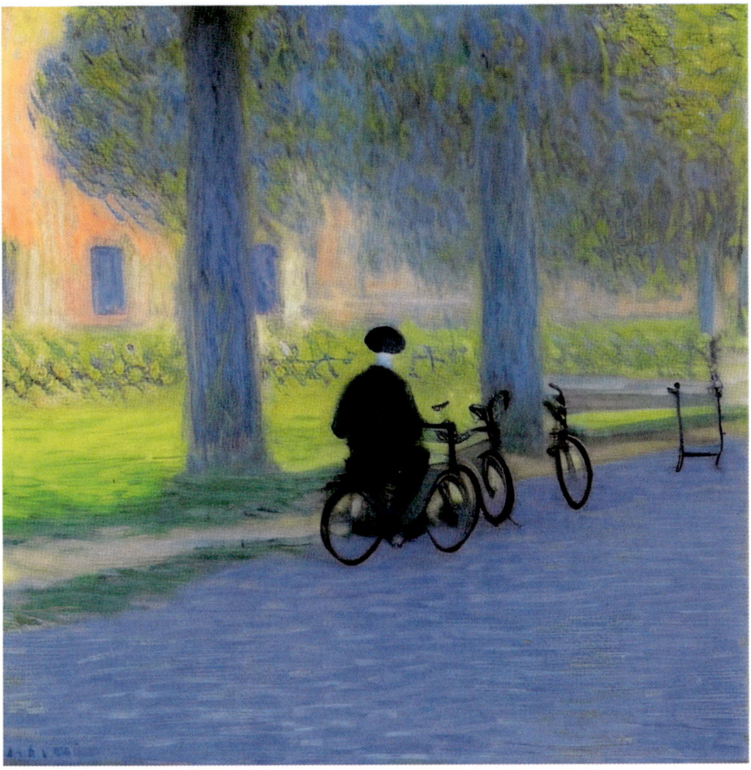

February 28(29) - Philippians 4:7

And the peace of God, which passeth all understanding, shall keep your hearts and minds through Christ Jesus.

Lord, we thank you for the peace that passes all understanding. Help us to keep our hearts and minds focused on Jesus Christ. Give us comfort in times of trial, and strength when we are weak. Remind us that your peace is always available to us, no matter what struggles come our way. Show us how to share the peace you give us with others, so they may know of your love and joy. In Jesus's name, we pray, Amen.

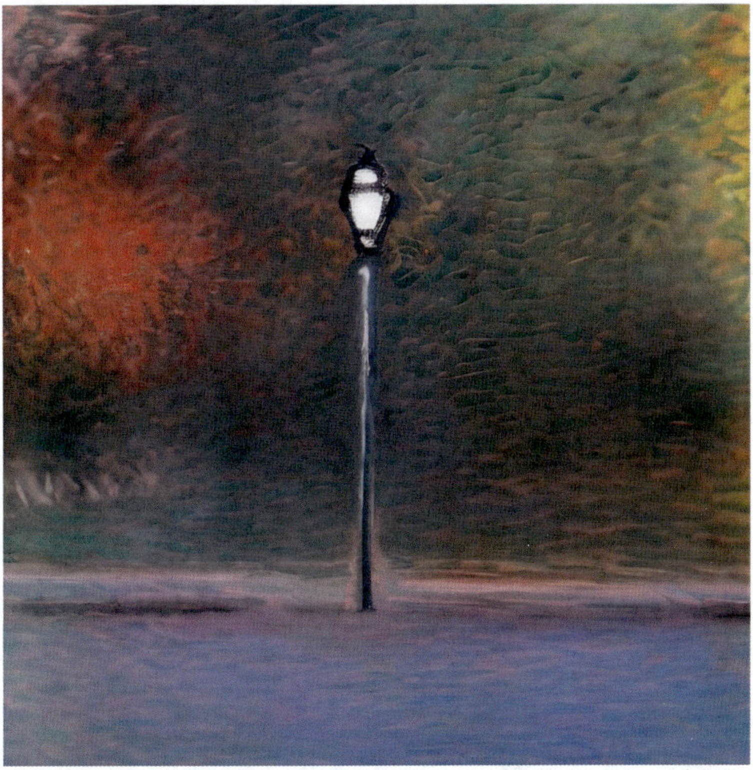

About the Author

Bill L Sherley is a data solutions manager, programmer, writer, and minister. He has seven dogs: six rescues and one beagle who rules the house. Bill loves spending time with his family and friends, going to church, working on computers, and of course taking care of his rescued animals. He writes poetry, fiction, nonfiction, and religious books.

Books in This Series

Daily Prayers and Bible Verses

The Daily Prayers and Bible Verses series is a wonderful collection of 12 books, each one providing an inspirational way to honor your faith and relationship with God. Each book contains meaningful scripture, prayer, and art; to give you the guidance you need throughout the year. Spend time in daily devotion with these inspiring prayers, verses, and images to deepen your spiritual connection. This series will help bring greater peace, joy, and strength into your life as you praise God!

Daily Prayers and Bible Verses – January

Daily Prayers and Bible Verses – February

Daily Prayers and Bible Verses - March

Daily Prayers and Bible Verses - April

Daily Prayers and Bible Verses - May

Daily Prayers and Bible Verses - June

Daily Prayers and Bible Verses - July

Daily Prayers and Bible Verses - August

Daily Prayers and Bible Verses - September

Daily Prayers and Bible Verses - October

Daily Prayers and Bible Verses - November

Daily Prayers and Bible Verses - December

Books By This Author

Christmas Paganism

Made in the USA
Middletown, DE
06 December 2022